SPEAKING FORTH
GODLY CHILDREN

Influencing the personality and
character of children yet unborn.

DAVID TREASTER

BALBOA.
PRESS

A DIVISION OF HAY HOUSE

Scripture taken from the King James Version of the Bible.

Balboa Press books may be ordered through booksellers or by contacting:

Balboa Press
A Division of Hay House
1663 Liberty Drive
Bloomington, IN 47403
www.balboapress.com
1 (877) 407-4847

Because of the dynamic nature of the Internet, any web addresses or links contained in this book may have changed since publication and may no longer be valid. The views expressed in this work are solely those of the author and do not necessarily reflect the views of the publisher, and the publisher hereby disclaims any responsibility for them.

The author of this book does not dispense medical advice or prescribe the use of any technique as a form of treatment for physical, emotional, or medical problems without the advice of a physician, either directly or indirectly. The intent of the author is only to offer information of a general nature to help you in your quest for emotional and spiritual well-being. In the event you use any of the information in this book for yourself, which is your constitutional right, the author and the publisher assume no responsibility for your actions.

Any people depicted in stock imagery provided by Thinkstock are models, and such images are being used for illustrative purposes only. Certain stock imagery © Thinkstock.

Print information available on the last page.

ISBN: 978-1-5043-7911-3 (sc)
ISBN: 978-1-5043-7912-0 (hc)
ISBN: 978-1-5043-7913-7 (e)

Library of Congress Control Number: 2017906846

Balboa Press rev. date: 05/16/2017

In honor of
Rev. Katrina Ornelas
Senior Visionary of
The Center for
Practical Spirituality

San Antonio, Texas

Contents

Foreword

I'll never forget when I first met David Treaster. He was playing the keyboard at the Center for Practical Spirituality (C4PS) when I walked into the sanctuary. As I looked at him, I just knew inside me that he was someone very special – someone who was going to make a difference in the world I lived in. It was as though a spiritual light was emanating from him from the inside out. I made a note that this was someone special. I told myself I would like to get to know him.

As I've grown to know David, I've found he has many divinely inspired messages to share to help improve our world and our future. When I found out he had a spiritual encounter as a child, I knew my first impression of what I picked up was a correct intuitive impression.

I encouraged our Reverend Katrina Ornelas to invite him to speak and give the sermons or lessons at C4PS once a month. Rev. Katrina trusted that intuitive lead. Since then, David has blessed us with so many of the teachings that help make life a pleasure to be a part of here on earth. I feel the experience he has gained speaking at C4PS has prepared him to be quite the accomplished speaker and, with his heart, to go out into the world and share his messages with others. I foresee him to be a world renowned author and speaker accepting many invitations to come to your area to present a life changing message that you will treasure.

I see David as an accomplished author even though this is only his first of many books to come. His greatest passion is explaining his messages through his writing. This book, *Speaking Forth Godly Children,* is the unveiling of his initial message to us in print. After reading David's book, I'm convinced it is 100% divinely inspired and has something to do with the spiritual experience he had as a young child.

You will find David's writing easy to read and easy to understand. His examples are so relatable to our lives. He thinks of every possible situation for the unborn and addresses how to handle the simple techniques that he offers.

The beauty of *Speaking Forth Godly Children* is you can take David's message about many of the practices unveiled, and you can apply them to other "children". As I like to say, "to your babies" which could mean anything that becomes your baby. That could be your special projects, your home, your relationships, your job — you name it. You can take the messages and apply them to your everyday encounters and your everyday "babies".

I have first-hand experience with the simple principles that David has outlined in this book. When he mentioned something about his book during one of his sermons at C4PS, I shared the positive impact it had on my life and my prayer life. Others attending C4PS took note and have begun to put David's techniques into practice. We have all seen amazing results. Be ready for a life-changing way of living life when you read *Speaking Forth Godly* Children. Even if you don't have children, you can greatly benefit from applying the numerous messages spelled out throughout the book.

Most importantly, David gives us hope and inspiration for future generations to come. I personally have had concerns about the future of my unborn grandchildren and descendants to come. After reading what David has presented to us, I no longer worry or fret for their future.

There is a way explained in this book that will put you at ease as it has me.

If everyone would follow David's practice, we would never have to be concerned about our decedents' futures. May you read David Treaster's *Speaking Forth Godly Children* and put his techniques into practice for the child you wish to bring forth into this world to change this world we live in for the better.

One last thought - I so hope you have an opportunity to hear David Treaster speak in person. Every time he speaks, he openly shares divinely inspired insights. Those insights, brought forth in an easy to understand way, help you with your everyday life so that you may truly live life to the fullest. That in itself can change your way of thinking and your way of life will be richer!

February 5, 2017
Daisy Thames
Lead Associate Visionary
Center for Practical Spirituality
San Antonio, Texas

Introduction

You have seen it happen. I have seen it happen. Frequently we hear it happening before we even see it. We are at a store and hear a huge commotion in progress. Standing there is a parent and in front of the parent at least one child. That child is either standing or lying on the floor. Through their cries, yells, screams, tantrums and possible body flailing that child has a message for the parent. I want something and you are not buying it for me. I want you to buy it RIGHT NOW. The parent standing there often has a look of embarrassment. Nonverbally you can tell they wish they were anywhere but here. And normally we are all glad that it is not our child having the tantrum.

That parent is wishing they knew the best way to end the spectacle. It is also probable no one taught them about the techniques taught in this book. No one ever told this parent that they could choose and affect the character of their child. No one ever told them that they could influence their unborn child in ways that would make parenting much simpler and much more enjoyable. No one told them that they could have a child who is a help and blessing to the world for as long as that child, and later as an adult, is living and is active on this earth.

The parent in this scenario had parents and grandparents who also did not know these truths and techniques as shared in this book. They all just thought the personality of their child was the luck of the draw. They thought that you just have to accept whatever kind of child you get, whether for good or otherwise. They just assumed that your child's personality is just a happenstance. They didn't know you can ask God for a child who blesses and helps this world, who is even a world changer, for the good. They didn't know you can request a good natured child who loves spiritual things and who helps the world through spiritual means.

All the standard wisdom of what is normal in childhood and in child-rearing has many of us believing so called "truths" that may not, in fact, be really true. Facts like, every parent can just expect the "terrible two's". No getting around that one. (Oh, really!! My wife and I debunked that so called inevitable truth.) Or the so called fact that every child will have many, possibly strong, problematic discipline issues. (We didn't in our home.) And so, on and on. I will share in detail what DID happen in our home so you can judge for yourself.

This example parent, their parents and grandparents, didn't know that the time to stop or head off such a dramatic display of negative self-will (as described in the first few paragraphs above) starts way before that child is born. In fact, steps can be taken even before conception to set the course for the personality and character of the upcoming child.

This book shares the true story of how my wife and I did just that with our child. I have since discovered others that have used similar techniques with their children, also with great results. As you read you will now learn and know how to set the course for a new child. You will learn how to receive just such a sweet spirited "blessing" child who also blesses others and the world. You will learn how to influence the personality and character of a godly child, a child as yet unborn. You will learn how to call such a child to the earth to raise as God's abundant blessing to you, and to the whole world.

Chapter 1
The Foundations

In order to best understand the methods that I describe in this book, it is best to first know a bit more about this author. It is also good to know how the methods were formed and how they originated. It also helps to know the stepping stones of knowledge that influenced the development of these methods. That way you can best understand the spirit and intention I have in writing this book.

I was a happy smiley young child. I showed a strong sensitivity to spiritual things at a very early age. When I was six years old my parents took me and my younger sister to a gospel concert at a large church. I enjoyed the trio in their performance. Then at the end they talked. After the concert was over and we were driving home, I asked Mom what they were talking about at the end. I didn't understand the words and concepts they were conveying. Mom explained it was an altar call for those who wanted to live right and be in communion with God. I immediately decided that I wanted to be in communion and fellowship with God. So, in the car at age six I chose to pray a "sinner's prayer". I was neither encouraged nor pressured to do so. I simply wanted to be "right with God".

That same summer within about two to eight weeks, I distinctly remember a very significant event. I had a childhood book titled <u>God Is Love.</u> My reading skills were limited. I could read the title and some of the words in the book, but not very many. I was in my room lying on my bed. I tried to read the words in the book but mostly just couldn't. So I thought about the title of the book and what it meant, for forty-five minutes. I didn't know the concept or the word "meditation" at the time, but I was meditating at age six. I had no teaching in meditation, but I was doing so naturally and instinctively. (I learned the concepts of meditation, formally, many years later.) I was simply a happy six-year-old child who loved God and meditated for forty-five minutes. I was in relationship with God to the extent that a six year-old can be, and perhaps just a bit beyond the abilities of an average six year-old. That meditation event made a very powerful memory imprint in my young brain. That memory is the fact that God truly is Love. That fact is a memory that remains strongly to this day.

As I grew, I deeply loved going to church. We went Sunday morning, Sunday evening and many times Wednesday night. I loved praying at the altars, singing the songs, and hearing the spiritual teachings. I absolutely hated children's church. I got MUCH more out of the adult church sermons. I felt a true connection to spirit and to God at church. I could discern that connection. Those interests continued all throughout high school and into college.

During my college years and into early adulthood, I went to Charismatic and Pentecostal Christian churches. During that time, I learned a lot about connecting with Divine Spirit. Of course, they used the words Holy Spirit or even Holy Ghost. The important factor is that I became good at quickly sensing God's Spirit and connecting with Divine Spirit. That is an extremely important fact in the formation of this book and its techniques. Without that knowledge I would never have received the leadings from God that formed the processes of speaking forth godly children.

After graduating from college, I learned about the power in the prayer of agreement. That is when two or more people agree on a specific item or group of items to pray about for a specific outcome. By having multiple people praying together and adding their faith together, they strengthen and intensify their prayers. Subsequently, I learned about masterminding and noted the strong similarities in the two techniques.

In the three years immediately after college, I did much studying of Biblical passages. I learned about the patriarchal system of culture which typified Old Testament biblical times. Men were the rulers and head of households. Women were considered owned objects much like cattle. Children were also owned by the men. That fact was a major factor in the use of dowries in arranged marriages. In more modern marriage that was the reason for the phrase, who gives this woman in marriage? Originally the father answered, "I do.". The polite answer was modified to "her mother and I".

I also noted the importance of a father's blessing and their use of a double inheritance for a first born son. The biblical account of persons even trying to steal a blessing was noteworthy. Along with the blessing came wealth, status, importance and community standing.

While learning these various cultural aspects, I decided which I believed were good for today's times and which aspects I felt were best left in the past.

I further learned about the power and importance of the spoken word. God has given humans creative power similar to that of the Godhead. Just like God, we can use words to create and bring things and circumstances into manifestation. In the Bible, Romans 4:17B KJV says God "calleth those things that be not as though they were". Elsewhere in the Bible, like in Genesis 1:3 KJV "God said, Let there be light". Over and over in the KJV book of Genesis, the phrase "God said" tells how God spoke the worlds into existence. When the words are spoken, the items declared do not yet exist in physical reality. But by using spoken words, for example prayers, in faith, or by using spoken affirmations with believing, humans can also call things and circumstances into being. God placed that gift and power of speaking things into existence in every person.

I remember the phrase "What I think about, I bring about". (I do not know who originated that phrase.) Our thoughts are also very powerful. When we focus our thoughts in prayer and/or affirmations, and especially when we speak those thoughts, well, we super-empower those words and thoughts. That fact is most important in the techniques I teach in this book.

I have also noted the tremendous effort humankind has spent learning to use and control that creative power of words and the tongue. Despite the occasional frustrations experienced by some of us along the way, it is not rocket science. It is so simple that we tend to make it much harder. Our thoughts AND our words, ALL of them, are just like the paddle in a canoe. As you handle those thoughts and words, you steer your boat, your life course. You alone control your paddle. You alone monitor and control your thoughts and words. The preponderance of those thoughts and words WILL control your path.

Here is one other foundational truth. The words we speak towards others can affect the thoughts and words of others, and what they think about themselves. What becomes the thoughts and words of others will affect THEIR lives. As we each live our lives, we affect the lives of others. We help to raise and pull them up, or beat them down. We choose if we will bless others or curse others. I think we already know we need to bless and encourage all others.

Additionally, I have learned much about the interaction of our spirit selves to our physical body and our human brain. Many persons confuse their spirit mind, which is within us, with our physical human mind. The two are distinct and have separate functions. Yet they are connected very closely and normally function with great synchronicity with each other. So much so, many people confuse them as one entity. For example, the spirit mind never sleeps. The human brain and thought processes DO sleep. I have a relative who rarely uses an alarm clock. That relative says that they "program their mind" to wake them up. Your spirit is alert and awake as you sleep. For example, your spirit knows what "time" it is as you sleep. Your human brain and mind is asleep and unaware of the time. Basically what this relative had mastered was setting an order with her spirit to wake her up at a set time. She thought it was her "brain" waking her up. Actually, she was tapping into spirit to be her alarm clock. She was highly practiced and skilled at this technique. That is just one example of the separateness of spirit mind versus human brain mind. Later in this book we will touch on that topic again.

Then, most of all I MUST acknowledge God and the Divine Spirit. The Godhead prompted me to pray for our developing baby. The Spirit took pieces of teaching and knowledge that I had in my physical mind and in my spirit. The Divine One wove those thoughts together. Creator God truly taught me what to do and in some cases, why. Those promptings and Divine instruction formed the techniques now disclosed within this book. When God teaches you something, you still have free will. You can act on that knowledge or just ignore it. Sometimes to act on what God reveals takes effort, extra "work" or what may seem like extra demands on your time. In my case, I am SO EXTREMELY GLAD I followed God's instruction and teaching on this topic. I am so glad God used me and my wife to pray over our developing baby. I am glad that we spoke forth a godly child.

All of these foundations will be touched upon and explored in this book. These studies and observations and foundations have all heavily influenced the methods and techniques that I teach in this book. These foundations informed the methods and techniques I wanted to use with my child. Naturally my wife was of a similar mindset and we agreed to use these methods together in unison and unity. These foundational studies all guided the formation of the principles used, and revealed here, for speaking forth godly children.

Chapter 2
Pre-Natal Spiritual Preparation

My wife and I were three and a half years past college graduation. I had a B.A. in Accounting (with honors) and also Computer Science. My wife had a triple major and went on to earn a Master's Degree. We both worked outside the home.

My first two years out of college I worked at a CPA firm doing computer audits and traditional audits. After two years I changed jobs and worked as a Data Processing Manager and first in-house computer programmer at a spiritual ministry.

We had planned to wait five years after college before having children. But at three and a half years after college my precious wife was desperately yearning to be a housewife, loving and raising a child. Because of her training, she is highly skilled in researching. She researched what we should do nutritionally to prepare for conception. The only two items I can recall are Folic Acid for her, and Vitamin E for both of us. There were some other supplements that I fail to remember. We also prayed about what else we could do to best benefit our child. My wife also did more research on the variety of ways we could best care for and prepare for our baby.

After we conceived, our next step was to insure our baby had the very best prenatal care possible- physically, mentally and spiritually. We arranged for a medical group with many prenatal/baby doctors along with a nurse midwife. In fact, the nurse midwife had delivered more children than each of the doctors, despite being an amazingly young woman. It was not unusual for her to deliver three to five babies a week.

My wife did many things to seek to benefit the baby. She talked to the baby, played music to the developing child, and prayed over our coming child. My wife structured her activities. She added some and subtracted others, to maximize the benefit to the baby. Throughout her pregnancy, my wife absolutely loved being an expectant woman. In fact, after our baby was delivered she cried because the wonderful pregnancy period was over. The child was now outside of her physical body.

There were also the spiritual preparations. As soon as we knew we were expecting, we formulated our spiritual action plan for our miracle (i.e. our baby). That plan resulted in seven to eight months of nearly daily action to affect our baby's spiritual makeup, personality, and character.

First we started by defining the personality characteristics and spiritual characteristics we desired for our child. I recall that we took several days to draw up the list of characteristics we wanted for our child. We sought God for guidance and my wife and I talked intently, seeking to develop the best list possible. We wanted the maximum and best benefit for our child, and for our child's entire adult lifetime. After finalizing our list of characteristics we started implementing our plan. The first day of implementing our spiritual action plan, we both placed our hands over the developing child. I spoke on behalf of us both, per our agreement, like this:

"Creator God, thank You for our growing child. Thank You for blessing us with a child to live in our home. Dear God, we <u>ASK</u> for a child with a good spirit, a child who loves God and who loves spiritual things and is sensitive to spiritual things. We <u>ASK</u> for a child who is smart and loving. We <u>ASK</u> for a child who excels, who cares about people, and a child who seeks You. We <u>ASK</u> for a child who is merciful and gracious. A child who forgives and is a blessing to others. We <u>ASK</u> for a child who excels in school. Who helps the needy and less fortunate, a child of Light and Love and Sunshine and Joy and Happiness, a healthy child.

Thank You God. Thank You for giving us this child with these gifts. We thank and praise You God. Amen, and so it is."

We believed we could affect our child's personality and character. Our "speaking forth" became a daily event. We returned the second day, placed our hands over the developing child and **DID NOT** ask God. Instead we approached God with a sense and attitude of gratitude. We spoke nearly the same words on day two, like this:

"Creator God, <u>Thank You</u> for our growing child. <u>Thank You</u> for blessing us with a baby for our home. God, we <u>Thank You</u> for a child with a good spirit, a child who loves God and loves spiritual things and is sensitive to spiritual things. We <u>Thank You</u> God for a child who is smart and loving. We <u>Thank You</u> for a child who excels, who cares about people, a child who seeks You. We <u>Thank You</u> for a child who is merciful and gracious. Thanks for a child who forgives and is a blessing to others. We <u>Thank You</u> God for a child who excels in school, who helps the needy and less fortunate. We <u>Thank You</u> for a child of Light and Love and Sunshine and Joy and Happiness, a healthy child.

Thank You God. Thank You for giving us this child with these gifts. We thank and praise You God. Amen, and so it is."

Day after day we placed our hands over the developing child and repeated the words we spoke on day two. Thank You God for a child who is .... Essentially we spoke the same thank you pronouncements, in gratitude, every day for seven to eight months. Notice that we only ASKED God one time, the very first day we spoke forth over the child. From day two on, our speaking forth was a celebration of thank you's.

Notice, we did not beg or plead with God for what we desired. As the children of God, the people of God's own creation, we DO NOT need to plead or beg or bargain with God. It is God's great pleasure to give us our heart's desires. And most times, I do certainly believe that the Godhead planted our desires in us in the first place.

So, we only ask one time and then celebrate with thank you's each day thereafter. This point is very important. A key is that we spent the entire pregnancy praying and speaking over the developing fetus, our growing and developing child. Those daily moments of speaking over the child were daily moments filled with great joy and filled with love for the child. Daily, my wife and I grew in love for each other and our thoughts swelled with great expectation of our coming baby.

Chapter 3
The Results

Our daughter was born in the summer of 1984 weighing almost ten pounds. She was just a bit "small" for my wife's family. They tend to have ten to eleven pound babies, usually delivering two to three weeks "late". Our baby daughter, and later as a toddler, was an easy, happy, joy-filled child. We totally missed out on the "terrible two's". Instead we had the "terrific two's". Our smiley sunshine daughter made child rearing an easy joy. You know how many toddlers will color the heck out of one or more books? Our daughter made a single line mark with a crayon in one book just one time!

At about age three, we prepared for a major move across four states. My wife and I were getting rid of excess items in preparation for the move. Our daughter understood what we were doing and why. We talked with her about a riding toy she was outgrowing. We simply told her she was about to be too big for it. The toy was rated for children eighteen months to three years old. We were trying to prepare her for its upcoming removal from the items to be included in the move. On her own initiative our daughter said "I want to give it to [so and so]", one of her friends from church. So that is what we did.

Our daughter also had a very large cardboard playhouse in her bedroom. I believe the box had been for a console TV. My wife had cut in a door and a four-paned window, created a pitched roof, and had painted the playhouse to look like a lovely cottage. Underneath the window were painted flowers in a painted flower box. The playhouse was just too large and fragile to include in the move. We told our daughter, in advance, we would have to leave it behind. Again, she presented the solution. "I want to give the playhouse to _____". The family named was an apt choice. They had two young children, a boy and girl about 3 and 6 years old. They also had a large, mostly empty basement, with plenty of space to play. They joyously accepted the gift.

My wife and I were a bit concerned that later our daughter might cry and miss these two toys. But that never became an issue. She never looked back. She never spoke of the riding toy or playhouse again.

Discipline was never a problem in our home. Our daughter was so sensitive that one stern look would cause her to burst into tears! The vast majority of the time we had a happy atmosphere in our home.

In early elementary school my daughter quickly established herself as an excellent student. In first grade a female classmate suffered the death/transition of her mother. Our daughter displayed a precocious caring, understanding and empathy for her classmate. Our daughter wanted to attend the funeral. My wife was advised by funeral professionals that it would be inappropriate to have such a young non-relative attend. However, the school phoned my wife. They told her that our daughter was talking much about the situation and seemed very fixated on the funeral. The classroom teacher and principal of the school strongly recommended that she attend.

In discussions it was arranged that the principal and classroom teacher and our daughter would ride in one car to the funeral service. There she would join my wife, and the two would sit together. After the service our daughter again rode in the same car with the principal and her 1st grade teacher. For transition and decompression, they took her to get an ice cream cone. After the cone was eaten they proceeded back to school. Our daughter seemed very satisfied to have been permitted to attend. I was very impressed with the school's handling of the situation.

Even as an early elementary student, our daughter was an extremely precocious child. She always acted like an adult. At this point, my ex-wife and I lived several states apart. (My wife and I had divorced.) My ex-wife had to intentionally, and with much planning, create events where our daughter could truly experience life as a child. I also had to do the same thing for the same reasons when my daughter came to visit me. That is, as her parents we had to help her experience her childhood with normal childlike wonder and childlike emotional responses. Shortly after such a planned event ended, she would revert back to adult reactions and responses.

A year or two later my ex-wife came across a man writing a math course for schools. He needed some students to test the curriculum. My ex-wife arranged for our daughter to be a test student one night a week. As a result, our daughter became accelerated in math beyond her classmates. The classroom teacher and school principal picked up quickly on this fact. So our daughter was placed in the math class one grade level above her grade level. That remained true each year through high school graduation. That meant two years she had to be specially bussed to a different school building for her math class. All that was done, without complaint, by her public school system.

Our daughter seemed to have an unending thirst for knowledge and learning. The breadth of her interests for learning was amazing. Also, there was a piano in the home. She learned a number of things about playing piano. She loves to sing. She had an interest in several musical instruments. The instrument that caught her attention the most, and by a large margin, was the cello. The cello became her signature instrument all the way through high school (and beyond). Of course, she loved playing cello concerts for family and friends. She has, to this day, a strong love of music and also of spiritual music and worship music.

At a young age she also demonstrated a loving nature. In this case with pets. There was a cat in the home. Later an indoor pet bunny rabbit was also added. Our daughter trained the rabbit to use a litter box just like a cat. In fact, she trained the rabbit so well, it became a free range pet inside the home, being locked in its cage only for nighttime sleep. Naturally, caring for pets teaches responsibility and giving love and caring for another besides one's self. Our daughter soared at these tasks and skills.

Our daughter also displayed a great love for drawing and art work. The walls of the home were continually filled with art work. The selections were constantly being switched out as new drawings or painted works were created. More and more art just kept coming. This was a great outlet for her creativity.

As a form of summary, she thrives on variety. That trait is true for both her mother and father. (My love of thriving on variety is really pretty high.) But our daughter has that trait to an even higher degree than either of her parents.

Around late elementary school or very early middle school, my daughter had a microscope. She prepared slides of the pollen she had collected from at least 75-100 plants. She studied the slides to compare the shape and characteristics of the pollen. She noted how the pollen of related plants tended to be similar, versus the vastly different looking pollen from other unrelated plants. This study was done for fun and recreation. It was in no way a school assignment. At the time, I did think how very precocious and noteworthy.

Throughout her school years, report card time nearly became a standing joke. Every time her report card was a list of A's. It was a standard joke line of "well, no need to look at her grades. They will be the same as always". Actually looking at the report card was always just a bit anti-climactic! That is the kind of non-drama every parent wishes to experience.

At graduation, our daughter was the valedictorian. She also set a new record grade point average (GPA) for her public school system. She achieved a GPA of over 5.0 on the 4.0 grade point scale. Such a high score was due to the number of advanced placement courses and college level courses she took in high school. At her graduation she had an asterisk next to her name in the program noting her as valedictorian. The commencement speakers were chosen by competition. Our daughter was not chosen to speak. Her achievement as valedictorian and school record high GPA were also not announced. She simply walked across the stage and received her diploma exactly like every other graduate in the school that year. (Yes, as her Dad, I was not happy about those facts. Can you tell? I had always been very impressed with her public school system until then. But I CAN say that her school system did a very good job of educating her. Overall, I should have no complaints.)

In preparation for college, our daughter took the SAT exam (a scholastic aptitude exam. That test is used by colleges and universities in the United States to aid in student entry decisions). She achieved a perfect score on the math section of the SAT exam. My wife was a good student. I was a good student. But our daughter blew us both away with her school victories. It seemed that with her, one plus one equaled three, or four, or five!

For college, our daughter decided to study Astro Physics. She chose a tier one research university for her Bachelor's work. Then for her Master's in Astro Physics, she attended graduate school at a top five program. Her initial goal was to get a Doctorate in Astro Physics and be a professor teaching Astro Physics. But she decided that there must be a greater purpose in life than debating theories in physics. As a result, she did not start her doctoral studies. Instead she entered the job market.

In speaking forth and praying for our godly child, before our daughter was born, we had asked for a smart child who was a good student, a child who excels. <u>WHAT AN UNDERSTATEMENT</u> ! My wife and I had received SO much more.

After finishing her Master's degree, our daughter worked on her "MRS". She dated a law student while she was in grad school, and continued dating him after finishing her Master's degree. They were married. She helped to put him through law school. He finished his degree, passed the bar exam, and was admitted to the Bar in his state. He then started practicing law. As an adult our daughter did quantitative analysis (QA) for a manufacturing facility of a Fortune 500 company. Quantitative analysis is a complex math technique used in business settings to minimize costs and maximize profits. For my daughter's employer, QA was used to maximize product production, schedule duration of a particular product production versus another product, and to schedule workforce needs and hours of production line usage for profit maximization and cost minimization. Her calculations were used by the plant manager to oversee and manage the operations. That's our daughter! Eventually she came to dislike the hours required by that job. She left that position to become a substitute school teacher. But she does more than teach. She invests herself in the lives of the students, but in a professional way.

Our daughter's thirtieth birthday was in 2014. She spent the day in a recording studio playing cello tracks for a female vocal recording artist just to help out that artist. So our daughter spent her entire special day seeking to help and bless another person. But the vocal artist will bless many people with <u>her</u> vocal talents. So, in a way, our daughter spent her birthday blessing a cascade of many other people.

On the Saturday following her birthday, our daughter and her husband drove two hours to where they wanted to celebrate her birthday – a 24-hour-a-day prayer center. They spent several hours there in prayer. Later my daughter told me, "Dad, it was so much fun praying at the prayer center". She declared it was a wonderful birthday celebration. Did she choose a big party, or a big dinner, or a special night on the town? No, she chose to pray for others. I find that remarkable. (But of course, I'm her Dad.)

Bottom Line- our daughter is EXACTLY the person, without one single exception, that my wife and I declared we wanted. Our daughter is exactly the person we spoke into existence on this earth. A caring, loving, compassionate helper of people, who loves spiritual things and is a force of love in this earth. We spoke many things over our developing fetus. We manifested and received a daughter who is an exact match to our affirmations, prayers and thank you's to God. We spoke forth a godly child.

Chapter 4
A Fluke ?

Were our results a fluke? I have many reasons to say "No". I know of other persons who have done similar things with similar results. I will share one particularly telling example because of the contrasts it presents.

When my daughter was four, I moved back to the area where my wife and I had previously lived. I was good friends with a local attorney. The attorney and I were about the same age. Sometimes we would lunch together at a local restaurant. One time during our lunch conversation I mentioned about praying/speaking over our daughter for spiritual and personality characteristics. I also told the results we had received.

My attorney friend told me that he and his wife had done the same thing, speaking and praying over their first child. Again, they had done this as their child was growing and developing in the womb. Their results were the same as ours. A good spirited, a good natured child who was easy to bring up. Then his next statement shocked me and deeply saddened me. He said that during their second pregnancy, they were busy getting his law practice set up and established. He said they forgot to pray and speak over the second child. (Both were girls.) And the result with their child number two? Their second child was strong willed in a negative way. She continually challenged parental authority. Bottom line, she was very challenging to rear and bring up.

Many religious belief systems agree that Creator God made humans after the nature and abilities of God. God gave us creative, manifesting abilities just as God used in creating this world and universe. That is why our spoken words are so powerful. I know that many people probably already know these truths.

Basically, we know the power of spoken words, the power of spoken affirmations, the power of the prayer of agreement, the power of faith and believing, the power of masterminding, etc. If two or more people routinely speak, believing, over a growing unborn child, it is sensible to believe those acts will have positive results.

I think we all know that efforts spent in speaking prayers and affirmations are not wasted words nor wasted minutes. When the result desired is achieved, we truly need not be surprised or shocked. Results from our efforts is what we do expect. Those results are WHY we say the prayers and affirmations. Why should we ever be surprised at God answering all of our petitions and desires? We should not ever be surprised.

I have had several other friends who spent time praying over their children as they were growing in their mother's womb. They also achieved wonderful results. Loving parents who invest time, prayers and affirmations over their children yet to be born can expect good results.

After the experience of my wife and myself, and the experience of my attorney friend and his wife with their two children, and the positive experiences of other friends, well, I can only conclude that our combined results were NOT a fluke. The results were, in fact, exactly what we should expect. To quote an animated cartoon character "there's pow'r in them thar words".

Chapter 5
What Is The Deal?
The Steps Revealed

So, what is the deal? Just this. I believe any two or more people can use these techniques. Why two or more people? Because of the principles of the prayer of agreement/master-minding. I believe people can speak the personality characteristics of their child, grandchild, niece, nephew, etc. in concert with that child's parents. They can totally influence the character and the personality of the developing baby. In fact, I believe they can begin even before conception and then continue throughout the pregnancy. And I believe they can significantly make child rearing much easier and more enjoyable as a result. My wife and I did it. Some of my friends have done it. And you can do it also.

For many centuries people have tended to believe that we have to just take whatever kind of child we receive, carte blanche. Most of us were not told or taught that we can specify characteristics of our children. But we don't have to just accept a luck of circumstance child. We can let our desires for the type of child to be made known to God and manifest such a child.

Let's review the important points of using this technique to speak forth a godly child.

First, Identify the characteristics of the godly child you desire. Seek God, the Divine, to guide you to wise choices for your child's personality and character. Connect with God's voice and direction. God has a much broader overview in this. Pray and seek the characteristics and personality traits God desires for your child.

Sometimes people say "I don't know how to hear from God". That is not true. Each person is born with the ability to hear from God. In the beginning of the book I shared examples of how I heard from God as a six year-old. I shared how, as a child I longed to go to church. I loved being in the presence of God. Many people have not received good instruction on the topic of hearing from God. I say trust your intuition and "gut feelings".

These are methods of spirit communication. The more you practice using and acting upon your intuition and gut feelings, the more skilled you will become in hearing the voice of God, the instructions of Divine Spirit.

Scientists have yet to figure out how intuition works. They don't yet know how to measure and detect spirit. I have heard people say, "I don't know how I knew that. I just knew it". A strong deep knowing without any other explanation is likely Spirit seeking to communicate to you. You can practice receiving those messages and thereby turn up the volume and increase your sensitivity. Trust your intuition. Act on your intuition. Do the same with your "gut feelings". The more I trust and follow my intuition, the more readily I receive reliable guidance that way from Divine Spirit.

Dreams are also another vehicle of spirit communication. Your spirit never sleeps. Your spirit is awake and communicates with Divine Spirit as your body and physical mind sleeps. I used to think I didn't sleep much at night. I went to a sleep study and found out I actually was sleeping twice as much as I thought. I was SO aware of my spirit mind that it seemed like I was awake when I was actually asleep. I was aware of "thoughts" that were occurring at midnight, 1 am, 2 am, 3 am, etc. The sleep study, however, showed that my physical brain wave activity was in a state of sleep. I was misinterpreting my spirit being activity as physical brain activity and thought.

Some of you may be confusing the two also, spirit mind versus physical mind. Your spirit is awake and active and communicating with Divine Spirit even as your physical mind is asleep. To increase my peace of mind concerning sleep, I have learned to pray and affirm that my sleep is sufficient and fully healing. I spend no time worrying over thoughts of insufficient sleep. If you think you have sleep issues I recommend such an approach to you. Check it out medically if you want or need to. But do not worry over sleep. Daily declare you sleep well, and your sleep is sufficient and restorative.

As an aside, I have a prayer and affirmation that I like to use when I go to bed to sleep. (Prayers and affirmations seem so blended to me that I like to call them "prayfirmations".) This sleep prayfirmation is based on Psalms 3:4-6 in the Old Testament KJV Bible. "My sleep is bliss. My sleep is blest. God keeps me safe and gives me rest. My sleep and rest are fully restorative. Amen and so it is." You are welcome to use this prayfirmation if you so choose. Use it as a springboard to wonderful, Divinely empowered, rest filled healing slumber. I encourage you to say it out loud so your mind thinks it, your brain also receives the message through your hearing, and then your brain digests and performs that command. Say it out loud two, five, ten times or more. I suggest saying it after getting in bed and just before starting to drift into sleep.

In seeking spiritual wisdom and guidance from God through dreams, look at the dream. Is it just a negative, nasty, horror? If so, that likely came from human mind, not Divine Spirit. Throw that dream away and forget it. BUT if a dream leads to a deep seated knowing that can't be explained by any other method, there is a strong chance Spirit is on the line. Also if a dream occurs multiple times, pay closer attention to that dream. Pray and ask Divine Spirit to reveal the message in the dream. A recurring dream has a stronger possibility of containing a message from God. Again, practice will increase your spiritual sensitivity.

Another method for hearing the Spirit of God entails the use of meditation. Both sleep and meditation are ways to get the brain in or through an alpha brain wave state. A person can more easily receive from spirit in the alpha state. At that time, the brain is not cluttered with many competing thoughts. Yes, meditation is a classic method for humans to receive from Divine Spirit to your spirit.

So in choosing the characteristics for your child, I encourage you to include spiritual characteristics. I believe it is very important to seek God's wisdom multiple times to clearly get the mind of God when working on the characteristics list. This is a process that should not be rushed. I am quite sure you want God's highest and best for your child. Plus, I believe we all want our child/children to be adequately equipped to fulfill the life mission God has for our child/children. Much attention to God's guidance helps to assure that we do truly receive God's guidance.

Be open to the purpose God may have for your child. Some children are here by God to be the indigo children. You may be selected to parent an indigo child. Just stay open and seek and receive God's wisdom for your child's best and highest good and blessing. Remember God sends them here to bless and help the world, and to fulfill THEIR life mission.

I want to STRONGLY discourage trying to select and specify the gender of the child. I also STRONGLY discourage earthly parents from trying to specify the vocation or life mission of your child. God has a breadth of vision and knowledge that humans do not possess. God's purposes might be for a girl for a specific reason, OR for a boy for a specific reason. Allow God to send the gender of child that the Godhead needs here on earth. AND similarly, God is the giver of a person's life mission, not humans. Divine Wisdom knows what is needed, when and where. Most of the time those details are far beyond a parent's imagination or even wildest dreams. Allow God to slot the life purpose for the child. Don't include the vocation or life mission in your daily speaking/prayers over the child. If you wish, you could pray and affirm, "we receive exactly the right girl or boy as God has selected. God sets our child on the right paths and they will bless this world and fulfill their life mission. Amen and so it is".

Next, use the centuries and centuries old classic spiritual method of Asking, Seeking and Knocking. That method is an excellent method to use to call your child to earth. It summons your child to earth filled with the characteristics that God has revealed to you. Call them to earth with the personality and character that stays in your heart and soul as the best for your child. Do it in this way:

Day One- ASK God, Universe, Divine Love, Divine Spirit for a child with all of your chosen characteristics. We only need to ask once. We never need to beg or try to force God or resort to bargaining. Our loving Creator God desires our very best and seeks to give the best. We simply need to ask. As the Bible says in James 4:2c (KJV), "ye [you] have not because ye [you] ask not". Our part is to ask, to speak, in faith and love, believing that we receive.

Day Two and until delivery- THANK God, Universe, Divine Love, Divine Spirit for a child with your chosen characteristics. Remember, there is MUCH power in living in gratitude. That is partly why we don't want or need to beg or bargain with God. It is God's good pleasure to grant our requests. Universe conspires to give us what we desire, if it is for our best and highest good, and harms no other person. Persons who live in gratitude immensely please Creator God. Remember to speak believing in faith, that what you speak is destined to come to pass.

After delivery of the child- Enjoy the results of your preparations and labors. For my wife and I, we thoroughly enjoyed our daily prayer/speaking forth sessions over our child. It did not feel or seem like work. Those moments were daily pure joy. I predict you will find it so also. Revel in the joy and potential ease of raising your baby and child to adulthood. Declare that your household is an abundantly blest household. Live each day expecting, believing and receiving God's very best for each of you.

Chapter 6
Ask, Seek, Knock in Gratitude

In the Bible, in Matthew 7:7-8 (KJV) Jesus is teaching. He says: "Ask, and it shall be given you; seek and you shall find; knock, and it shall be opened unto you." These are extremely basic and fundamental spiritual principles. These principles comprise the very essence of the act and practice of prayer. These principles are also foundational to the act of manifesting. Yes, these principles are the bedrock of the methods used in the act of speaking forth godly children. These principles are well known in the Christian world, and also generally well known in other spiritual systems. Ask, seek, and knock are foundational, transcending, universal and powerful spiritual principles. We all should be using them frequently and often.

Before asking, we must first decide what characteristics to ask for in our child. That determination can take a concerted effort in itself. I strongly recommend asking and seeking God for Divine Guidance in creating the list of characteristics for your child. Know and believe that Creator God plants desires in us as God wills. We become tools and vessels of God bringing forth God's will in this earth. Ask God what God desires in our child. Believe that Divine Mind truly reveals what we need to know, and plants those desires in our heart. God is the true source of our desires.

After deciding what characteristics we would like in our child, we use prayer and spoken words to ASK Creator God, Universe, the Divine One. We use this spiritual principle of asking. By asking we bring our requests before God. We ask for the specific characteristics and personality traits that we have purposed in our hearts, realizing that God is the actual source of our desires and our list of characteristics. Asking is what we do on day one in speaking forth the godly child.

I teach that we need ask only once, on day one. Some may ask, why not ask many times. The answer lies in three words: seek, knock, gratitude. By combining spiritual methods and techniques, such as seeking and knocking in gratitude, a more powerful, synergistic result can be achieved. Some persons may ask what I mean by synergistic. Simply stated, synergistic means a more powerful result. A synergistic result is a result more powerful than many would expect. Synergy is where one plus one equals three, or four, or five. We only need to ask on day one because we will move on to seeking and knocking. We will do so with gratitude. Once we ask on day one, God already knows the desires of our hearts. In fact, God knew our desires before we did, because those desires actually came from God. Why do we want to seek and knock with the additional of gratitude? Think about it this way. Let's consider child one. How many times has a child been heard, "I want a candy bar. I want a candy bar. I want a candy bar. I want a candy bar. I want a candy bar, and I want it now!" And on and on. The adult has already heard the request and knows the desire. Now let's consider child two. What happens if the child says, "I want a candy bar. Thanks Mom SO much for all the wonderful things you do for me. Thanks for treating me with a candy bar today. I love you Mom. You are always such a blessing to everyone around you."

Well which child do you predict receives their desires? That example helps to typify why we need ask only once. Starting day two and thereafter, we seek God and knock on God's door daily. We seek and knock in love, with gratitude. Thank you God for a child with this character. Thank you Divine One for a talent of such and such. Thank you for............ as we go through our list of attitudes and characteristics and personality traits and talents for our child.

It is important to stress that we are not seeking to manipulate God. But we are using the spiritual principles of seeking and knocking. Seeking implies a continued effort. Normally we seek until we find what we are looking for or achieve our desired result. Knocking tends to imply multiple attempts. Rarely does a person knock on a door only one time. Knocking is usually a multi-time event. And by using gratitude when seeking and knocking, well, it is like the very best icing on the cake.

Universe loves and responds to gratitude. Gratitude is a very high powered, high energy vibration activity. Grumbling and complaining have a low energy vibration. The Bible declares that God dislikes grumbling and complaining (see Numbers 11:1 KJV) but loves a cheerful heart filled with gratitude, love, thanks and caring. (See II Corinthians 9:7 KJV) These latter items (cheerfulness, gratitude, love, thankfulness, caring) are all high energy vibration attitudes and actions. We are wise to use the higher energy vibration actions in speaking forth godly children. We are wise to use the most powerful spiritual techniques. By adding gratitude to your prayers and manifestation efforts you are adding extra power to your efforts. It is truly like supercharging your requests and desires with a high powered spiritual resource that magnifies your energy and effort into the fulfillment of your desires. We declare our thanks to God for the results we desire. We fill our hearts with love and anticipation of the good things to come. We fill our hearts with gratitude to God for the bountiful, wondrous answers to the desires we speak.

So, on day two and thereafter we use seeking God daily by knocking, seeking and thanking God for the answers to our asking (which occurred on day one). We seek and knock with gratitude on day two, and each day thereafter, until our child is born into this world. We combine seeking, knocking and gratitude to achieve that mega high powered, high vibrational result. It is spiritual activity at its best. We don't do this to try to manipulate God. First of all, God cannot be manipulated. And secondly, to try to manipulate God is simply wasted time and wasted activity. Instead, we use the spiritual principles that the Godhead uses and that God established. In the biblical account of creation, the record states that after God had created the world God examined what was accomplished. God expressed a desire and then looked at what was accomplished. God said "it is good". God expressed an appreciation and a gratitude for the wonderful results. I personally believe God was in a state of thankfulness at the beginning, middle and end of the creation process. Like God, we use these principles of asking on day one, of seeking and knocking in gratitude on day two and each day thereafter. We use powerful spiritual principles in a right way, to lovingly and thankfully, speak forth godly children.

Chapter 7
The Real World

We live in a real world. Our world is not a Polyanna world. Everything isn't like the homogenous perfect television families of the 1950's and 1960's. Those television families tackled huge disasters like a burned roast with company arriving in minutes, mixed-up crossed messages, confused identities, a runaway pet, etc. All these huge catastrophes were fully fixed and resolved in 30 minutes. The end of each program left the viewing audience feeling all warm and fuzzy and content. All seemed right with the world.

By contrast, our world can become a bit complicated. Coping with the opportunities present in daily modern life can challenge even the most poised, confident persons. We can all use tips and help in navigating this life. I want to take a moment and explore how speaking forth godly children can be affected by this very diverse world.

EXAMPLE ONE

Recently I was talking with a woman about this book, just before it was to be sent to the publisher. She was very excited about the book. She said she wanted a copy of this book. Then she asked, is it too late for me and my husband? I asked and she explained. "I have had 13 miscarriages including the ten times one of my externally fertilized eggs (from me and my husband) have been implanted. All of these pregnancies have failed. My husband and I are determined to have our own biological baby. We will not adopt".

I was astounded at their tenacity and determination. She said they were getting ready to do another implantation of a fertilized egg from her husband's contribution. A mutual friend told me they are using a different doctor and clinic this time. She wanted to know, is it too late for me and my husband to use the principles in your book? I replied, definitely not. (You know, in life, there are no coincidences, only Divine appointments. That is true for her and for me, and for us all. As a result of meeting her, I felt a need to make a last minute addition to this chapter.)

I said to her, start today. Say out loud, ten to twenty times a day "Thank You God that my fertilized egg attaches and grows into a wonderful, healthy, normal baby who is carried full-term and delivered normally." I told her, don't just think it. Say it out loud so your ears can hear it. Say it two or three times. Two to three hours later say it again. Repeat that process several times throughout the day. Get a sister or friend to join you saying it in your behalf. Get other friends to join you. Enlist Mon and Dad and Grandparents. Have them say it out loud several times each day. Keep saying it after the implantation until you receive the confirmation that the baby is attached and growing.

She smiled a huge smile. Then after that news, keep saying out every single day "Thank You God that I carry this baby full-term. Thank You God that I deliver a proper weight, healthy, breathing and fully alive, totally normal baby, without defect." Get your spiritual support team, your sister, friends, parents, grandparents to join you saying these prayers and affirmation daily. Have them say these things everyday wherever they are, wherever they live, near or far.

She was such a positive spirited person. She became very excited and said, "I am going to start as soon as I get to my car". I, the author, have a mutual contact person to this woman. I am so ready to hear her reports as they come in.

If you are a woman who has had one or more miscarriages, be encouraged. Bring Divine Spirit into the equation is a strong proactive way. If you decide to try another pregnancy, join the woman above in praying and affirming. "Thank You God that I carry this baby to full term. Thank You God that I deliver a proper weight, heathy, breathing and fully alive, totally normal baby, without defect." Get others to join you. Be a team to speak this baby into the world.

I know a woman who had three miscarriages, and the doctors told her to stop. The experts told her you can't do it. You can't have a baby. She persisted in trying and the fourth time she delivered a baby daughter. After that she delivered a son. The "experts" are not always right. God has a say in these things. We enlist God's supernatural spiritual powers as we pray, live right, and invoke Divine God's help. Be encouraged.

EXAMPLE TWO

Let us consider the case of a single woman who becomes pregnant as a result of abuse or physical violence. The events that occurred were not planned. The pregnancy was not expected. In all likelihood, the man involved has fled her life. He is not planning to assist in any pregnancy and is not interested in raising the child. For this example, let us assume the woman has decided to carry the child to term. Is this woman and child excluded from the techniques taught in this book? Absolutely not!!! Are they excluded from receiving God's blessings? Again, absolutely not!!!

First, this woman needs much love and assurance from those near to her. She needs to know that God loves her and wants her very best and highest good. She needs to know that her child is special and very important to our world and also to God. She needs to receive a lot of support and love from the people around her. She also needs to feel assured that she is fully qualified to speak over her child and give this world her very best gift – a godly child.

The methods in this book use the techniques of the prayer of agreement or the concept of masterminding.

That requires two or more people. So the woman in our example needs to find one or more persons to join with her. Potential agreement partners could be her mother or sister or best friend or a worship center co-worshipper or father or uncle or...... well, the list is nearly endless. They need to get together in person or by phone and agree as to the characteristics that they will call forth daily. I strongly recommend that they make a written list of the desired character traits, personality traits and spiritual traits. That agreement is critical. They must be on the same page in their efforts and understandings.

Once the agreements have been settled upon, then the daily prayer events begin. Of course, the first day is asking. Day two through delivery is thanking God. If at all possible, praying together in person is best. If that is not possible, then doing so on the phone or via Skype or other live streaming method with each other is the next best choice. In person or by phone, each participant feels that they are part of the team. They give to each other and receive emotional support and develop the assurance that they are a team together. For the woman in our example, emotional support and partnership are especially important. We all need a knowledge and sense that God loves us and is with us. Our woman here especially needs that love and knowledge. By praying together daily and making the affirmations, not only does she receive support, but they together make progress together in speaking forth a godly child.

Of course more than two persons can participate. I would encourage enlisting other persons also, including persons in other cities, states or countries. The long distance partners can join in daily prayers and affirmations towards the same goal and end. True, they cannot participate in person at the same physical location. Instead, they become part of the extended team. They just need a clear and definitive list of the characteristics that they will all be agreeing upon for the child. Each day for the duration of the pregnancy they will be affecting the development of the growing child, bringing into reality the desired person. All of them together are part of the team, asking once, and then seeking and knocking daily, in gratitude.

EXAMPLE THREE

Next, let's consider two married or partnered women who intend to have a child with the services of a sperm bank. Just as the woman in the prior example, God loves these women and desires the very best for them and their child or children. They are not excluded from using these techniques. They can also expect positive results.

They, like any hetero couple, can begin before or after conception. Whenever possible I strongly encourage beginning before conception. When starting before conception, the formula remains the same. Agree upon the desired personality characteristics, personality traits, and spiritual traits. Enlist other persons, local and long distance, as desired. Let all know the traits desired and agreed upon. Everyone ask God on the first day and thank God with true gratitude on day two and thereafter through the birth of the child. Daily believe that the child prayed for or affirmed is truly received. Remember, God is Love and Love is God. God also wants your best possible child and is thrilled that the parents and friends are exercising authority in the earth concerning the child.

EXAMPLE FOUR

A couple, hetero or same sex, seek to use the services of a surrogate in bringing forth their child. Just like in example three, I would recommend using prayers and affirmations very early in the process. First, for God's guidance and direction for deciding upon and arranging the surrogate. Also for prayers and affirmations for the child as outlined in this book. The Godhead most assuredly understands the very great longings for a child that this couple feels. God knows the struggles they've experienced in reaching this point and decision. God loves all the persons involved so very much.

These persons are candidates for speaking forth godly children just as much as anyone else. Their child or children deserve this type of start as much as any other child. They will need to decide upon the characteristics they want in the child. Then they can arrange the persons who will join them in their daily declarations. The first day of speaking forth their godly child they will ask God, and on day two and thereafter they will thank God. Their circumstances change nothing else whatsoever. All parents and parents-to-be are welcome to use these techniques. I believe that God is pleased when they do.

EXAMPLE FIVE

Now let us consider the situation of a couple, again hetero or same sex, who are planning to adopt a child. Some might say that changes everything. I disagree. Those who say it changes everything might say, in an adoption, the child to be adopted is possibly already born. Maybe, maybe not. I believe such a distinction might be a moot point.

Nearly all humans understand that on this earth time is a horizontal line. Yesterday already occurred, today is happening now, and tomorrow is what will come and what will be. Some Metaphysicians believe that for God time is vertical, not horizontal. All is now. Even the Bible has several verses that support such a view. The Old Testament revelation of the name of God to Moses, in Exodus 3:14 KJV, is "I Am that I Am". This instance of God's name is not I Was or I Will Be, but always "I Am that I Am". II Peter 3:8 KJV declares that with God, a thousand years is as a day, and a day is as a thousand years. That makes no sense to humans, unless they view that statement in the context of vertical time. In both cases, scriptures declare today is the correct time, not yesterday and not tomorrow. I think that in God's realm, time is vertical. It's all NOW.

So if time in God is vertical, the question of whether a child to be adopted has been born yet or not becomes irrelevant. The couple wanting to adopt simply needs to start immediately to decide upon the characteristics of the child they want. They need to start immediately to speak forth their godly child. They should ask God for the desired characteristics on day one and thank God with true gratitude on day two and until their child is in their hands and care. They should do all this believing that God is well able and willing to give them the child they seek. They must believe that God gives them the desires of their hearts. They should trust that God is more than able to handle time issues. God knew they were going to adopt long before they did. God can, and I believe, will make all to happen, correctly, in Divine timing and in Divine order. The adopting couple is able and qualified to participate in speaking forth their godly child.

Here is the bottom line. All parents and parents-to-be, regardless of circumstances, are able and welcome to speak forth one or more godly child or children. Every child they have should be given this level of care and preparation before they arrive. No parents are excluded or shut-out. God desires for all to prepare for their baby this way. The parent-child relationship is enhanced. Child rearing becomes even more fun and fulfilling and rewarding. And I believe behavioral issues and discipline issues are greatly minimized. All parents are welcome to speak forth a godly child.

Chapter 8
The Children Already On Earth

I am quite sure some parents are thinking, thanks for telling us all this now. One might say, my child was born last year. Another says, we have two children, ages 3 and 6. Another parent declares our children are in middle school and junior high. A different parent says our five children are all already born and here on earth. A final set of parents says their children are all adults and they are now having their own children. All of these parents agree that they and their children didn't get the benefit of what is described in this book. Now what are we to do, these parents ask?

First of all, you must remember, you have not come upon this information before now. So don't for one second feel, or be tempted to feel, any sense of guilt or wrongdoing. No person can do what they have not been taught. I most certainly believe that God never expects us to act or behave beyond our knowledge. So, first, be at peace.

Next, start from a place of peace and hope. Getting all tangled up in worry, care, or a sense of hopelessness does not serve you well. Negative energy does not give birth to positive energy. In fact, it will hinder and complicate your tasks and goals. Don't allow yourself to be hindered by negatives. We all get fast, better results by starting in the positives. Remember to relax. You, yes, you- take a deep breath. Center yourself with God and Universe. Believe that positive results are possible. Believe that you and God can do anything and accomplish anything. It is true. A positive you and God are a winning duo.

I assume that you wish a child or 2 or more children had some different personality characteristics or spiritual interests from what you normally see. Those desires are likely different from child to child. I think most of us would agree that different children often have unique and different personalities. So spend time seeking God and Divine Spirit. Get Divine guidance on how to proceed. Acquire wisdom before proceeding. A slight delay to infuse yourself with Divine wisdom is time well spent. Afterwards you are well equipped to proceed.

Can you agree that prayers are a worthwhile and beneficial activity? Can you agree that affirmations are likewise a worthwhile and beneficial pursuit? If you can agree to one or both of these statements, then the next answer begins to become clear. Start using prayers and affirmations now, even immediately, to affect, influence or change your child or children. Know that your efforts are worthwhile and positive, even if you see no evidence of that truth. If possible, get one or more persons to join with you. Again, agree upon what you are going to affirm or pray concerning. Remember the great power of agreement when praying and affirming. **Ask** God on the first day and then **thank** God on day two and forward. I firmly believe that as long as I am living in a human body on this earth, my earthly prayers and affirmations are never a waste of time. The same is true for you.

Realize that since we are talking about persons who are alive and well, their free will comes into play. The older the child is, the more their free will may be an influencing factor. I do not say this to discourage you. Quite the contrary. But do be aware that their free will can add to the amount of effort you may need to expend to accomplish a desired change. The amount of time required for the transformation might also be longer. If the child is a fully grown adult, the prior two statements can be especially true. Remember, however, that nothing is impossible for those who truly believe. So whether the child in question is 2 years old or 7 or 12 or 16 or 22 or 35 or 52, know that your efforts are not futile. One person at our worship center recently shared the true story of wishing her husband would quit smoking. She used prayer and affirmations for twenty years, but sometimes was tempted to feel it was hopeless. Then one day her husband, out of the blue, declared he was quitting smoking, NOW, cold turkey. And he did. That was over one year ago. So never become discouraged. Don't give that negative energy a place to roost. Dispel it immediately with positive affirmations and prayers. Over and over and over until you win.

Burn it into your thinking. Stay in the positive. Do not become discouraged or disallusioned if you see no changes as quickly as you would prefer. Perserverance pays off. The motto, Never Quit, applies here. Ask yourself, what is this desired change worth? In most cases the answer will yield the resolve to continue to pray and to affirm. Continue to speak those positive words, in faith, believing. Always remember, you and God are a majority. You and God are a winning combination. Get your agreement partners involved. Mastermind. Do so and if you don't give up, you will win. Conceive it. Believe it. Achieve it. Receive it.

Chapter 9
Being The Good Parent

My original thought in bringing a child into the world was for my child to have a good, very blest life. I also wanted my child to be a great blessing to the world. I did not try to dictate to Universe the details of what kind of blessing, or via what modality. I also knew that for these two goals to be achieved, I needed to be the best parent possible. I am quite sure that my ex-wife would agree that she also wanted to be the best parent possible.

I know that to be the best parent that I can be, it starts with my relationship with God. Starting at six years of age, I have always clung to "God Is Love". I have since expanded my view to: God is Love, and Love is God. Being very watchful about my interactions and communication with God has been a lifelong emphasis. I know at my core all other interactions with other people, including children, spring out from that most important base relationship to God.

When a child first arrives, life becomes very busy. Many times life with a newborn feels very hectic. Parents can feel swept along with all the needs and demands of caring for the new child. After a bit more time, the demands start to feel very automatic. Middle of the night crying means time to feed. Diaper change time fairly clearly announces itself. Feed. Change. Feed. Change. Burp. Rock and sing baby to sleep. Yes, within the first few months living begins to seem high demand and very automatic. Some parents begin to feel lost and maybe even overwhelmed. At these moments parents can begin to lose their bearings and sense of themselves. They can lose track of the long term goal.

In order to be one's best and bring up the child in an excellent way, the parent must remember to care for themselves physically and spiritually. A mother or father cannot give what they don't have. They cannot give out of their depletion. Moments of holding, rocking and feeding the baby can become moments of spiritual connection with the child and also Divine Mind. Those still moments are a perfect time to reach out to God's Spirit. What a blessed way to care for oneself while caring for the child. I assure you the baby's spirit will be touched as the parent holding them connects with God and Divine Spirit.

Remember to take moments to regenerate and connect to Spirit. Use whatever method works best for you to connect to Divine Spirit. For me, five or ten minutes or 20 or 30 to listen to good spiritually pleasant music quickly connects me to Spirit. Some may choose a special bubble bath. Meditation can be a good choice. In order to regenerate, you might wish to have that phone call to Mom, or a close friend. Do things to bless your spirit and to feel whole and well. At first it may not be easy, but do your best to care for yourself also.

Just as a mother who is breastfeeding is watchful about her diet and its effect on the breastmilk quality, be aware that what your mind takes in with books, movies, music, spiritual teachings etc. effects what you give out to your children. Make the inputs good and quality brain food so that what you feed your child in mental resources are good and wholesome, both to you and to them.

Similarly, our words to our children have such a powerful effect on them. I recommend we give our children wholesome, positive words and thoughts. Those words and thoughts build their character and mental health in very important ways. Our words and even positive mood and approach to life will likely be emulated in our children. They truly need a good healthy dose of positive words and positive life outlook. Your children receive those positive words and life outlook from you.

Similarly, we should introduce our children to positive interactions with God. I still remember that book when I was six- God Is Love. I wish I still owned that book. I remember many other positive, rich spiritual resources. Those included books, family trips to worship centers, movies, lessons in prayers and affirmations, parent/ child reading time and so on. Our spiritual investments in their lives are especially critical. A great spiritual foundation teaches Divine Love, that is God, and love and caring for others and treating others with respect and dignity. It adds the rights of others as well as our rights. It sets the tone for much of life to come.

Social interaction with other children is another important area of attention for the good parent. By playing with others and being with others our child's social skills are launched. I admit it takes effort and time to invest in social growth. Yet the process can be most fun, rich and rewarding. Birthday parties, sleep overs, a group ice cream store or pizza emporium event, camping, hiking and on and on. So many possibilities. Let Creator God guide you in the best ways to advance your precious child in social health and growth.

General life enrichment is another area to invest into your child's life. There are so very many ways to add spice, inquisitiveness, discovery and excitement to the lives of our children. Add some trips to various museums. Help them to see and appreciate art, and architecture. Play music in the home, and sing. Teach them to sing and play instruments. Have fun with a drum, tambourine, even plastic containers turned upside down as makeshift drums played with sticks. Teach improvisation and creating fun from little. Take trips to the zoo, go to sporting events. Encourage trying roller skating, ice skating, learning swimming, going camping and hiking. Teach about nature at state parks. Have them try various crafts, such as drawing, painting, collage, decoration, candle making, etc. The craft stores provide endless inspiration. Plan and take vacations and road trips. Make life fun, and exciting, Teach, by example, that this world is a place of endless wonder.

Ask God and thank God for guiding you on being the best parent possible. Do the same concerning your emotional responses to what the child does. That is especially true as the child grows. Live in Love, respond in Love. Seek God and Divine Spirit for help in those areas. Love is the best antidote and curative. We all need love, and our children need love and lots of it. By living, responding and being a constant conduit of Love we can be the best parents we can be. God has entrusted us with a precious life. Now we can be great stewards of that bundle of life. Set being the very best parent to your child or children as your goal.

Chapter 10
The Parental Blessing

In the first chapter of this book I briefly touched on the parental, patriarchal blessing, as described in the Biblical Old Testament. I want to expand on the more modern blessing topic now. In some sense, this could perhaps be considered an extra chapter. It does not deal directly with speaking forth a godly child during the child's time in the womb. This section deals with interactions with the child after the child has been delivered on the earth. This chapter concerns interactions with the child after the child is external to the birth mother's body.

First I need to cover the ancient topic of blessings and curses. What we sometimes hear called as "the ancients" had great intelligence and knowledge that is sometimes forgotten in todays "modern" world. Our ancestors back hundreds and thousands of years prior to today had a

71

good working knowledge of blessings and curses. Just the mention may conjure up images of witch doctors and voodoo. But that is not the case at the core of the topic. Witch doctors and voodoo are curses taken to the far extreme.

Our distant ancestors understood that when you spoke a good or kind word to people you were blessing them. Then at ceremonial times, an extra special blessing could be spoken. An example is the Old Testament patriarchal blessing where a father, advanced in years and possibly approaching physical death, would speak an official blessing over the oldest male child. Such a blessing would give them a double inheritance and patriarchal status in the family after the senior father's passing. These blessings were words of health, wealth, many children, financial increase and good standing in their community.

Conversely, they understood curses. Those were words filled with hate, loathing and vehemence. These words sought to harm, hurt, and punish persons the speaker felt had done them wrong. We have lost the understanding of curses. For example, anytime we might say to a child, you are a loser, or, you never do anything right, we have actually spoken a curse over them. Positive words have positive power. Negative words have negative power. Saying things to a child, like: you are stupid, or you always break everything, or, you stupid klutz, learn to pay attention, is placing a curse on the child. Repeated curses actually cause mental health damage and developmental damage. Spoken curses physically hurt.

I have some personal knowledge in this area. When I was in junior high school, a certain beloved male relative would take me hunting with them. First it was duck hunting sitting in a small boat on the edge of a lake. After that we would go to a local bait shop for a bite of breakfast. Then we would go quail hunting after eating. Before going inside the bait shop, that male relative would tell me "now when we go inside, you keep your mouth shut. I don't want my friends to see how ignorant you are." I knew I was practically a straight A student. But this relative didn't want his friends to see how lacking in knowledge I was about nature, ducks, hunting and such. I knew that if I was lacking in those areas it was because I had not been taught. This same event happened over and over. Those words stung like sleet in the face. Due to the repetition of those words and the event, a strong long-term memory was formed. Negative energy words are a curse and they create great damage.

I know this relative did not mean to hurt me. You see, he had not been taught about the power of negative words. He had not been taught the proper way to treat children, verbally. I dearly love this relative. Even at the time I knew the source and cause of those shortcomings. But those words did still hurt.

Now back to our main topic. After having done the steps to speak forth a godly child, it makes sense to keep the momentum going. There is a key activity that can help propel any child to even greater mental health, self-assurance and greater accomplishments in life. That is the life-long activity of parental blessings achieved with positive words that dispense positive blessings. Now the good news is other persons can also participate in giving the child blessings. However, it is especially important that the parents be heavily involved in a life style of giving blessings.

It is well known that the words spoken to any child can have a huge effect on the child. As a child grows and learns, it is essential those words be positive. The words they hear shape their self-identity and their thoughts about themselves. A heavy, heavy dose of "you are loved, you are good, you are able, you are a blessing, you are blest by God, you have many talents, you have many abilities, you will do great things, you are here to bless others and bless the world" is the way to start.

Many adults battle issues where the "tapes" or "voices" in their heads constantly repeat negative messages. Things like: you are no good, you are trash, you always fail, you always mess things up, you always do that wrong, you make bad decisions, I wish you were never born. YUCK. I cringe even writing such things. They are severely damaging. Children come to earth ready to have a big segment of their identity created by their parents and by other relatives, neighbors, other adults and authority figures. A precious life can be heavily damaged by negative messages. Negative messages can also lead to mental health issues and to developmental problems leading to that person having trouble living as an adult. It will also severely short-circuit what that adult can do to benefit all humankind.

If you, as a parent, have previously spoken lots of negative messages, forgive yourself. Pray and ask God to reverse and heal any damage you may have caused. Divine Spirit can accomplish many things. It is simply important to change NOW to positive messages to your children or adult children. Turn on the positive parental blessings immediately. God approaches us with constant unconditional love. That is our calling as human parents to our children. Give heavy doses of unconditional love. Use loving correction methods when correction or instruction is required.

God treats us with love and blessings. God is lavish in thinking positive toward us and giving us positive praise and words. It is Divinely in God's plan for us to do the same. Give verbal blessings to our children, to co-workers, to adult friends, to the homeless and poor and downtrodden. It is nearly impossible to give too much positive support. Be a beacon of love and light, speaking positive words filled with positive energy to all. God constantly does the same, to all of us!

Chapter 11
Son-In-Law, Daughter-In-Law

As our daughter grew and attended college I used the principles of asking, seeking and knocking in gratitude for another purpose. I was concerned about what kind of spouse my daughter would marry. I believe nearly all parents are concerned about the life mate their adult child selects. I am sure none of you are surprised that I used these principles to call forth a wonderful spouse for my daughter.

The whole process was basically the same. First I spent time seeking God and praying for guidance as to the characteristics I wanted to call forth in her future spouse. Now I am very aware that as an adult my daughter has every right to select the kind of person she wants. I choose to speak forth a spouse in a way that would not violate her choices but would simply enhance her choices.

Remember, as you can, to get one or more people to join you in agreement. Make sure you all agree as to the characteristics you all wish to jointly speak over the future son-in-law or daughter-in-law. Proceed with unity of heart and unity of spirit. Speak over the future spouse with an abundance of joy and of gratitude.

Once I completed the process of selecting the characteristics, I asked on day one. My asking went something like this. Creator God, I ask for a son-in-law who loves you and seeks you and desires to grow in spiritual knowledge and spiritual life application. I ask for a son-in-law who loves his wife, and that both my daughter and he would create a loving home where they would mutually choose to honor and respect each other and treat each other in ways that would please you, God. I ask for a son-in-law who does well in school and who obtains a good job and is well able to provide for their joint household. I ask that they would prosper and not suffer lack even as their souls prosper. Dear God, I ask that their children, however many they might choose, would be blest, happy, whole children, without physical or mental defect. May their children grow and learn in a happy, loving, blessing of a home. May my future son-in-law prosper in his wonderful job and receive recognition, advancements and promotions and abundant wage increases. May they both make sound judgements that are also pleasing to you God. God, I ask that they would fill their home with you God and with a love of spiritual things. God, may they help the people around them and be a physical and spiritual blessing to them. May they be used as the hands and feet and voice of God in the earth and bless and help humankind. I thank you God for the fulfillment of these requests. Amen and so it is.

Then on day two and thereafter I started seeking and knocking, with gratitude. Thank you God for a son-in-law who loves you and seeks you and desires to grow in spiritual knowledge and in spiritual life application. I thank you for a son-in-law who loves his wife and that both my daughter and he create a loving home where they mutually choose to honor and respect each other and treat each other in ways that please you God. I thank you God for a son-in-law who does well in school and who obtains a good job and is well able to provide for their joint household. I thank you God that they both prosper and do not suffer lack, even as their souls prosper. Dear God, I thank you that their children, however many they may choose to have, are blest, happy and whole children without physical or mental defect. Thank you God that their children grow and learn in a happy, loving, blessing of a home. Thank you God that my future son-in-law prospers in his wonderful job, and receives recognition, advancements and promotions, and abundant wage increases. Thank you God that they both make sound judgements that are also pleasing to you God. Thank you God that they fill their home with you, God, and with a love of spiritual things. Thank you God that they bless and help the people around them. Thank you God that they are a physical and spiritual blessing to the people around them. Thank you God that they are used by You as the hands and feet and voice of God in the earth, and may they continually bless and help humankind. Thank you God for the fulfilment of these requests. And I declare, Amen, and so it is.

So the thank yous to God continued and continued day after day until the time of their wedding. So now I am sure some of you are interested in the results. Well, my daughter and son-in-law were married in 2009. I had the joy of being present for their wedding in a historical setting with a very large also historic pipe organ. And yes, I put out the requests and thank yous, expecting

God to find and bring forth a husband of the nature I had requested. I am SO thrilled to say, YES, the asking, seeking and knocking in gratitude resulted in Universe finding a very wonderful man. I am so very pleased that he is a part of the family. I am thrilled that he is in my daughter's life. I am also thrilled that he is the father of my first grandchild, a grandson, who was born in 2015. As far as I can see and know, their home and marriage is just exactly as I prayed and believed for it to be. My son-in-law is exactly the blessing that I prayed and spoke forth in faith. Thank You God for Your blessings.

Ask, seek, knock in gratitude for your child and their spouse or life mate. Bathe that future coupling with spiritual blessing and faith filled belief. Creator God is a God of great and wonderful blessings. Just like that King James Version Bible verse, James 4:2c "ye have not because ye ask not". All we need to do is ask, seek and knock in gratitude and our Divine Parent will pour out wonderful and great blessings. Know your Heavenly Parent sees your heart and sincerity. Be assured that Creator God hears your desires, your prayers and petitions. Know that God WILL answer. I say, Amen and so it is.

Chapter 12
For Other Issues

By now it is probably becoming clear that these prayer and manifestation techniques do not apply solely to children, grandchildren, children-in-laws, etc. There are many, many other issues in life where these same principles can be used. For example, what about the person needing to find an apartment or a new home or residence. What about the student needing to select a college or graduate school. Then there are the people needing to acquire new transportation or a new vehicle. There is the person trying to decide whether to retire or keep working. Some persons have to decide whether to accept this job or that job. The next person is trying to decide whether to move to a different city or stay in this one. Another person is seeking God's protection and safety for each and every day. An entrepreneur is seeking to decide whether to buy or sell a business or whether to add or delete a product line. Another individual wants to figure out which brand of washer and dryer to obtain, or which dining room set. Then there is that lucky person that needs to decide which vacation venue they want. Along with that is the critical issue of which paradise vendor to hire. There is also the person seeking a spouse or life-mate.

All of these issues can be dealt with using the same principles set out earlier. A vast myriad of other issues can also be dealt with using these spiritual principles. The steps are identical. Seek the wisdom of the Holy Spirit/Divine Spirit. Ask for God's direction. Once you have decided what to pray for, then start on day one. Ask God for what you need and specify the details as exactly and clearly as you can. Then on day two and thereafter seek and knock, in gratitude. Thank God for the answer. Thank God for the specifics. Make it a time of thanks and praise, and yes, even of worship. Know that your gratitude adds miraculous power to your requests and speeds along the answer and fulfillment. You are combining the ancient spiritual principle of asking, seeking and knocking with the also dynamic power of gratitude. It is like a one two attack on the issue and a powerful release of the solution(s). Know that you cannot fail. Know that God will not fail you. Be assured that you will not fail yourself.

Allow me to share an example of a person wanting Divine protection and safety. On day one they pray: Creator God, I ask for your white light hedge of protection to surround me today. I ask that Michael the Archangel see to my safety and protection this day. I ask for the host of guardian angels to surround me as I walk, as I drive and as well for any passengers in my vehicle, as I work, as I shop, everywhere I go today and in everything I do. I ask that the guardian angels see to my safety, my vehicle's safety, my residence and to the safety of all my possessions. Thank You God for your provision of safety and protection. And so it is.

Then each day thereafter seek God and knock on God's door with gratitude and praise. Thank you God that this day you surround me with your white light hedge of protection. I thank you that Michael the archangel sees to my safety and protection this day. I thank you for the host of guardian angels that surround me and go with me as I walk, as I drive, as I work, as I shop and everywhere I go and in everything that I do this day. I thank you God that the guardian angels see to my safety, my vehicles safety, my passenger's safety, to the safety of my residence and to the safety of all my possessions. Thank you God. And so it is.

After I had shared about asking, seeking and knocking in gratitude with a friend of mine, they reported back on the effect in their life. When they first heard about this combination of spiritual principles, a "click" went off instantly in their spirit. So this friend shared how she modified her prayer for safety and protection. You see, even though she prayed foe safety and protection, a nagging worry hounded her and she was never totally sure she was really safe. After starting her daily thank-yous to God for her safety and protection a big weight lifted from her. Her trust in God bloomed and multiplied. She was able to go through the day in peace and in trust and contentment. Once when I was giving a spiritual teaching at The Center for Practical Spirituality in San Antonio, Texas, I shared this prayer/manifestation technique. My friend spoke up and told the people present how much using these principles had changed and transformed her life. Using the techniques had resulted in higher levels of tranquility and peacefulness. To that I can only add, may it also be so for you.

Chapter 13
The Vision

In the past few chapters I've discussed many topics. Those have included: The agreement of two or more people in prayer and affirmations, and Asking, Seeking, Knocking with and through Gratitude. I've included examples of real life situations that don't fit in a tidy gift box wrapped picture perfect and tied with beautiful ribbon. I've covered praying for children who have already been born and need ongoing love and Divine support. We have looked at issues of being the best parent (or grandparent) that we can be. I've gone over the critical importance of the parental blessing. We have examined ways to call forth a wonderful spouse for our child (children). I have even highlighted the many other issues that can be affected, influenced and turned to the best good by the techniques taught in this book. But now, let us focus back on the core topic of the book- speaking forth godly children. Think on how every parent can call to earth and manifest the best, brightest children, who would be the most able to bless and help and heal and positively change this world for its highest good.

Now imagine. Imagine a world where hundreds of thousands of people learn the techniques of speaking forth godly children. Imagine even millions of parents learning to speak forth godly children. Imagine a world with hundreds of thousands of parents using these techniques and calling to earth children to bless the earth. Imagine millions of parents all over the world acting on what they've learned and earnestly speaking forth godly children. Imagine what would happen in the world with so many people moving to bless and help others. Imagine a world where all those parents teach children in love and Godly wisdom. Imagine a world where millions of households use God's best and most loving child rearing principles to raise happy, healthy, well-adjusted, confident children. Imagine a world where such children become adults. Imagine that group of adults tackling world issues with Godly answers and resolve. Imagine those adults promoting win-win answers and solutions. Imagine a world with greater loving, caring, greater equality, and more humane treatment of the disadvantaged and the poor. I could go on and on. Oh my, imagine such a world!

What would happen if a largely unorganized grass roots network of millions who bless and help and love do so all over this entire globe. Yes, millions of people living to be God's hands and feet and voice of love and blessing all over this entire earth. Such a world is the ultimate vision of speaking forth godly children.

Such a world starts one child at a time. One set of parents at a time. One birth at a time. Such a world starts as each parental practitioner tells other parents and parents-to-be about the techniques they are using. Telling their brothers and sisters about their loving desires for their child or children. That world unfolds as grandparents and aunts and uncles and great grandparents are encouraged to join and participate in speaking forth godly children.

As we look at an imperfect world and horrible events, we can be tempted to be discouraged. We must not give in to discouragement. We are not helpless. We can bless and help and be God's people in this world. We are the voice and actions of blessing. Never allow darkness to extinguish or dim your light. Our lights shine brightly. As we all speak forth godly children, we continue working for God's best and highest good for all people. We continue working for God's best good for all this earth and all the earth's people.

Blessings to you on your journey speaking forth godly children. Blessings to you as you live as a part of God's wondrous answers for our age and time. Know that as we individually, and millions more just like us, do right things, the net result is absolutely huge. Yes, blessings to you, your family, your children and your extended loved ones.

Namaste.

Afterword

Every good building must have a good, solid foundation. Your prayers and affirmations (prayfirmations), provide an excellent foundation for the life and accomplishments of your child. You setup your child for a great life and wonderful success. God inspired prayers and affirmations give the world a new person who is best equipped to solve and cure the worlds evils and problems. You can be God's channel to bless the world. You can be a conduit of spiritual power for blessing others. You have the power to speak forth YOUR Godly child/children. By doing so, both you and your child/children WILL be a true blessing to this world. And so it is.

Printed in the United States
By Bookmasters